RAIN ON YOUR FACE

START THE REFRESHING PATH OF HEALING FOR YOUR INNER LIFE

By: Felicia Jamison

AROUND H.I.M. PUBLISHING

Around His Image Marketing And Publishing

ACKNOWLEDGEMENTS

I am grateful to You God for the spiritual guidance You give my life; Your word sustains me, Your power to heal has amazed me, and You are indeed a comforter. I desire to carry out Your calling to bring healing to others, and I want the joyful opportunity to express how excellent you are at healing our afflictions. You oh Lord CAN HEAL what "THEY" say is the worst emotional pain that can't be healed. Yes, you God can heal it all and cause us to stand free of any abusive behaviors. Thank you for the beautiful life I have.

I thank my mother, and sisters for their love as well as my circle of Christian sisters and brothers from RNCC. A deep thanks to Rick, Crystal, Coco, Anne, Nikki, Queen, Louise, Veronica, Lisa, Gloria, Vynedra, and Chaplain Linda; you are all examples of a true friend. Johnea, Gwen, and D. Doughty thanks for being a part of my education which gave me the financial independence to walk away. Liz thanks for showing me materials to heal and giving me roses at my award event. Ma Varel your love is with me.

I thank my spiritual parents Dr. Howard and Janet Morgan for teaching me my Jewish roots and the honor to be your Black Jewish Princes daughter. Thanks to my Pastors Dr Chapman and First Lady Sandie for standing by me in every season of my healing. Pastor David and Paulette Kean, Pastors Franz and Pastor Dianne of Church on the Rock, and Pastor Bruce CLF Kingston, Jamaica you all gave birth to my Ministry in Jamaica; deep love to all. Cathy Radlein sipping Blue Mountain coffee on your veranda over looking Kingston are treasured healing moments! Lorna thanks for your prayers and showing me how to love the children in Trench Town.

Deep thanks to my Jamaican spiritual sons and daughter: Gary your prayers fix everything every time, with your wife Carissa by your side, I get double love. Shawn thanks for reading scripture to me when I needed it most, your smile alone can heal anything. Alysia you are a joy to mentor, the glory of God shines from your face and Alysias, your husband, Odean makes me smile. I live to see you all shine and proclaim God's word.

Papa San (Tyrone) and Debbie you were family when I lost it all. God gave me the two of you, your kids to love me, Debbie's rice-n-peas and the sound of Gospel Reggae to bring back my joy. I thank the Messado family of Kingston, Jamaica for making me apart of your family, sharing your home and staff with me. Because of you I have a home in Jamaica that helps me continue Ministry in the land I love, my beautiful Jamaica. Having the added bonus of your Messado family love no words can express that privilege and your example of true love.

Isaiah 61 NIV

1) The Spirit of the Sovereign Lord is on me, because the Lord has anointed me to proclaim good news to the poor. He has sent me to bind up the brokenhearted, to proclaim freedom for the captives and release from darkness for prisoners.

7) Instead of your shame you will receive a double portion, and instead of disgrace you will rejoice in your inheritance. And so you will inherit a double portion in your land and everlasting joy will be yours.

BEAUTIFUL GIRL

Beautiful girl why are you so sad? Yes I'm talking to you…

Please listen you are the beautiful girl I'm talking to. Why do you think you can't make it? Listen to me; stop thinking those negative thoughts, because you can't die. No, no stop thinking about all that death and giving up. Beautiful girl live to see another day, just keep living, keep moving and you do have something to live for.

The path of death is not the answer for you. Beautiful girl don't think about the pills or any way to harm yourself. Beautiful girl you are lovely and there is a plan there is a way out of this pain. Beautiful girl, yes I'm still talking to you.

The evil words spoken to you are not true and the abusive actions you have experienced can end. Don't let the shame of another person's actions ruin your life. I care and so many other people care about you too.

Beautiful girl we will miss you if you go away, don't believe the lies we all love you and care about you. Please beautiful girl don't go, don't take your life live another day please. Beautiful girl tomorrow will be better please push past today's pain and I promise you healing is coming. God made you and God is right there with you ready to heal you and show the way to peace and true healing. Beautiful girl just rest take a deep breath, clear your mind and have no worries. God has come to heal the little girl in you, and make her whole again.

The dark shadow of abusive behavior is creating an illusion over you to feel hopeless. Don't worry if people judge you. Let them judge you while God is fixing it all. Reach out to another living soul for help. You are God's Beautiful girl….

Beautiful girl, I see your blessings and the bright future God has planned for you. Yes, you are simply beautiful. Beautiful girl, we are waiting to see the marvelous; healed you. So, reach out. Live on to see your purpose unfold. Rise up Beautiful girl. I want to hear that, you made it out of the darkness. I was in the same darkness. But, I got out of the darkness. I once was lost but now I have found the light; and so can you. You are God's Beautiful girl….Please come into the light of God's healing. You will look back at this sadness. It will be a small thing in comparison with the joyful days that are ahead. You will smile again. Oh! By the way beautiful girl, when you get out into the light, don't ever go back to the darkness. Remember get out. Stay out. Be wise…

RAIN ON YOUR FACE

A rainy day is seen by most people as a dreary dull day or it can be seen as day that you are alive to enjoy heaven's rain. After being divorced there were still legal issues over property, and funds to be settled. On a gray rainy day I was with my lawyer to do an out of court mediation to settle equitable distribution, but the day did not end in the closure I so desired and longed for. My lawyer looked at me with a gentle smile, and said well you still have RAIN ON YOUR FACE. You see my lawyer knew every abusive word, and gesture that had been done to me. Scott's words reminded me no matter what happened I was still able to feel the rain of that day on my face. I was alive!!

Women have lost their lives from acts of domestic violence or struggle to heal emotionally from mean spirited words. Rude aggressive words by a spouse are still in the category of domestic violence (I didn't know that before leaving home, I just knew it made me sad). Today, I am free of that, and the pain that those words caused me. Initially in my kind heart I could never understand why a human being wants to talk to another person with abusive words. With God's guidance I went on my own path to understand, and discover God's refreshing power to heal me. I am grateful for the days I can feel rain on my face and release the beautiful smile God gave me. Some people say silly things about abuse making you feel you ignored the obvious or you picked to be in the abusive situation. None of us would date a person who displays evil abusive behavior. The abusive person comes to you charming and kind displaying their best behavior. Part of your sadness is that this kind person has gone away and you don't recognize this person who is being so rude to you.

Professional women can feel so ashamed of being in an abusive situation and the judgment that people make about you. One of the many reasons I wrote this book is to give hope to women who are judged. Yes, you are smart and how did this happen? You often think what happened to the kind person you met? None of us have all the answers, but you need to have a clear picture of what is unacceptable behavior. Once you are clear on abusive behavior don't let that ever continue in your life or become a pattern of who you allow in your life. Clear this dark oppressive spirit from your life, and never let it back in your presence.

At the completion of this book I feel like I was never married. I feel like I never had one abusive word spoken to me. I stand amazed at God's power to heal me from the inside out. I feel like I'm twenty years old. I'm filled with wisdom. I hear God's voice quickly. I smile inwardly from sunrise to sunset. I feel fresh, clean, lighthearted, untarnished, and sound in my mind. I did the hard work to renew my mind and thoughts. This book will take you on a path to forgive, and heal. You will find no male bashing in this book. A good loving man is like a warm blanket on a cold day! This book is not about the exact details of my former spouse. I'm not focusing on the past. I am writing about being healed after loss, disappointment and overcoming the effects of abusive behavior. You will hear me say over and over, "You can't fix abusive partners." You can release them. You can pray for them. You can wish them a blessed life. Release them with an earnest prayer. Let go. Keep it moving. Now, the deep work of renewal is your only focus.

Remember a failed relationship doesn't mean that you are a failure. I am single, and whole like a beautiful rose. A single rose can be the center piece on a dining table releasing its unique fragrance, and set the mood for a delightful dining experience. I pray you will also become single and whole.

This book is a tool to help you with practical events in life. It will help you heal with the inner pain you feel after abuse and disappointment. I deeply desire for you to find the renewal needed for your life and new thought patterns. Every day will be a day you can grow and get new thoughts about life. You don't have to live in the world 'the abuser' tries to create over you. You may be alone, but you will be alive to find inner solace. No matter what your age; it's never too late, to experience God's healing over your life. Give no energy to the past, but use today's energy for healing. You are about to find the real you, and learn to make wiser choices to have an abundant life. I pray every day for people who read this book. May you be renewed in your emotions, inner thoughts, and don't look back look ahead. I promise you, your best and happier days are ahead waiting for your arrival.

DOING YOUR HOMEWORK TO HEAL

Commit to the Lord whatever you do and he will establish your plans Prov 16:3 NIV

Healing requires a strong determination that will challenge you and make you look at your fears. So now you need to make a strong commitment to your own life to embrace God's ability to show you the path of your healing plan. Read a topic daily to allow your inner healing and refreshing to emerge. Make it your special time of inner introspection with your favorite instrumental music playing, or sipping a cup of tea. If needed get up fifteen minutes earlier to have this time just for you to set your day. You will feel so powerful. Value your growth by making this simple adjustment. I am so excited for your journey of healing. Let the words in this book help you with renewing your thoughts and bring your cleansing rain…

1) Keep a pen and paper near to jot down your thoughts

2) Write down things you fear or goals you want to reach in the next 1-3 months. You must be willing to admit and recognize your fears/insecurities so you can heal in these areas.(Oh by the way everybody has some insecurity they are facing or overcoming) Fear is like moist mold in a dark environment, and it will grow into something ugly so give your private self exposure!! Remember fear is the hindrance not other people…

3) Read back over your thoughts/goals every 3-5 months. You HAVE to do this!! You will be amazed to see your growth and see you overcame the things you feared. You will say "was I scared of that"!! ??

4) Let your faith and expectation grow. Picture yourself new and whole. You set the stage of what healing will be for you. It really works…

5) Never do male bashing because that is unhealthy, and connected to areas of pain or bitterness. However; being clear on what abusive behaviors are, will put you on a healing path of freedom.

Use the following pages to write the fears you would like to release as well as the goals you are working to achieve.

FEARS TO RELEASE AND GOALS TO ACHIEVE

_____

_____

_____

_____

_____

_____

_____

_____

_____

_____

_____

_____

_____

_____

_____

_____

_____

_____

_____

_____

_____

_____

_____

_____

_____

_____

_____

_____

_____

WHAT IN THE WORLD WENT WRONG?

You can share your life with a person for 10 to 20 years, experience many days of joy, see them as your best friend, travel to adventurous faraway places together, and slowly that person's behavior can change into someone you don't even recognize. Take a moment and think about how your partner handles anger. If you notice anger management issues, don't minimize this behavior. It's one thing to have a little angry outburst however; it's a tragic moment when the anger escalates in an intense frequency towards you. At first you might think, "Well nobody is perfect. I just need to forgive them." This anger can come and go it can be gone for weeks or even months at a time. You need to beware when the anger is a problematic issue.

The warning red flag sign for you to look for is a cyclic pattern of anger, and your partner's verbal communication or actions will start to feel very hurtful. This anger is very toxic, and the next phase of this cycle will be intimidating verbal attacks. The cycle of these verbal attacks will become more frequent with the addition of some type of physical contact that is not loving or healthy. If someone ever tries to press your shoulder or a body part to keep you in a chair while they are talking, that is abusive. Your ears are working fine, and you can hear without this physical intimidating contact.

You may not get beat downs physically but, if angry rude words are being spoken to you this is wrong. The harsh words, glaring looks, cold hearted actions, and profanity are emotionally harmful. These anger filled words will kill something inside of you like a bullet kills its victim. When a person loves you, they will never harm you with their words or by their actions. They will not continuously hurt you or make you feel unsafe. Abusive actions should be left with God and the abuser, they are not yours to carry, fix or cure. (I will remind you of this frequently)

You may not be getting 'beat downs' or black eyes so you don't know to call it domestic violence. If a person's communication feels oppressive, insulting or disturbs your peace, well, guess what? That's abusive with a desire to intimidate you. A spring board is now positioned for other forms of abuse to occur. You need to get out. Find a safe place for yourself. Some church folks will talk to you about staying in the relationship and forgiveness. I will tell you get out. Find a safe place. Sure you can forgive the person, but domestic violence is a matter that YOU need to be protected from, first. I am a very strong Christian. I will share more later on forgiveness; but you need to be protected. Forgiveness is needed anytime we are in conflict with others. However; I feel a strong desire to reveal the need for PROTECTION, first.

Remember an abusive person lives in a continuous state of mind that feels inferior, and they are filled with an unseen internal dark personal torment. So they are displaying behaviors that are mere reflections of what dwells deep in their own heart. God deeply cares for them, and God will help them. I do not advise you to stay in a controlling unstable abusive environment, because you can't live a calm life in this inappropriate situation. Lastly, I want to tell you, their abusive words or actions are not your fault. Nor is their behavior something you adjust to or make excuses for. I will leave you with this mental picture. If you were profusely bleeding from a wound on your neck you can't go give another person CPR. Your primary focus is on your own freedom and healing.

NEW REVELATIONS AND SELF VALIDATION

Upon the personal realization that you are in an abusive relationship you may feel ashamed. It's because you didn't start a relationship with a rude abusive person. You will ask yourself how did this happen to me? Where did my nice kind partner go? Soon you will realize you have nothing to be ashamed of and you will be so grateful to be alive and strong enough to walk away from it all. You will value your purpose and seek a healing path and this must be seen as your primary goal for now. Another caution is to beware that people may judge you and look down on you when they realize you experienced domestic violence. Don't allow shame to rise up because of their judgments or questions.

I do scholarships for students in Jamaica and I had to let one of my students know why I was single. When I told her, "My marriage ended due to domestic violence." She said, "Oh boy and I always thought you were so strong!" I said to her "No, no Sheren it's the weak person who stays in the abuse but it's the strong person who leaves." Her eyes then lighten up with the new revelation. So I shout it out to the world and to any person who judges or attempts to judge us......THE STRONG PERSON WALKS AWAY FROM ABUSE. I will never allow the judgments of others to stop me from speaking truth and I don't have to feel ashamed in my new victorious life. When I am in the presence of judgmental people I am pushing my inner reset/delete button while they are in my presence talking!! Their behavior is not staying inside me because it's negative and unsupportive. They should start playing the 'Rocky theme' music or the marching band fight song you hear at a ball game. They should be celebrating you and expressing joy that you got out.

It is very important for you to surround yourself with healthy supportive people and good spiritual support. I also suggest no dating right away because you are healing and that needs to be done alone. Your healing should be you and God to get the clarity you need. I found a loving church with an anointed Pastor who has a strong healthy marriage and I saw this spiritual connection as the foundation of my healing. I also surrounded myself with family, my spiritual children in Kingston, Jamaica, my spiritual parents, friends and healthy love. Healthy love is so vital during your healing not a new dating relationship. The right people chosen by God's divine plan will be around you. The healing journey at times will feel lonely and so painful but the healing will come.

I had to find me again, and explore the true God planned purposes for my life. I do not think or suggest to any person that finding purpose/healing can be done in the arms of another man. A man can't validate you because you must first validate yourself! After obtaining this inner self validation, you can and will make wiser choices. Your discernment will also become very keen as you meet other people. There is an energy that comes from people and this is where you trust your instincts. You are not wasting your time on fruitless endeavors.

The new self validation you gain will come from a spiritual place so deep within you, it will cause you to see your great worth and what the real missing puzzle pieces of your life should look like.

Being alone for women can be very difficult, unfamiliar and not the norm that society dictates to us. So, if you are not careful, because of fear you will rush to the next relationship in an unhealed state of mind .Your unhealed mind will pick the wrong focus or the wrong man for your life. In other words, you will pick the wrong puzzle pieces to complete the beautiful picture of the life you are seeking. Early in life my Momma taught me sometimes in life you will stand alone when you stand for what is right and God is right there with you in that truth. My father Henry Jamison is deceased but his love was the first male love in my life. From my dad's love I learned that true love from a man is very supportive and protective. My father never hit me nor did he use profanity to communicate with me. I even remember one day my father told me he was my dad and my big brother. My spiritual parents Howard and Janet Morgan now call me beloved or chocolate princess; and they adore me. They taught me what a friend is to discern who I allow in my life. My spiritual parents recognized my gifts and talents. They always stood by me teaching me to seek the Kingdom Principles of God. Healthy Love is nurturing because it comes from God. My Jewish father Dr Morgan took his prayer shawl and covered me with it to pray as they called me their daughter. Real love is protective it never harms us. So all of the parental love I have had made me know I could stand alone and find validation inside my own heart.

IT'S TIME TO STOP CRYING

There are days when you just need a good cry. Get it all out. Let it go! However, you will know it's time to stop crying over the past. I will never forget the day I made the transition to stop crying and restructure my life. I knew my ability to gain control over my emotions would either make me or break me. I would say "nah we not crying about that." I began to see with God's help I was in control of my day, my thoughts, and yes my tears. It was just time to stop crying!! So I would look in the mirror and say you are so cute and you are not crying about nothing today. Then I would laugh myself silly because the strong side of me was taking over. The strong woman inside me takes no mess and has a big sense of humor. So as I stop crying I also started laughing more.

Women are very tender and sensitive because God made us with a unique tender sensitivity. This sensitive quality will cause a woman to care tenderly for her children and be a nurturing wife in her home. We should celebrate that we were wonderfully made by God with this lovely sensitive trait. However, we must be careful to not live totally in an emotionally sensitive disposition at all times. There is a time when the tears have to cease, because the tears become a distraction that might prevent you from moving ahead. So your tearful emotions can become a disturbance to you own personal growth and empowerment. Tears are very healthy in a grieving process and allow expression for painful experience to be released. However; there is a transition where tears evoke a gloomy mood. When this gloomy mood occurs it's time to deal with facts and stop the tears.

So look at the facts connected to your tears and yes write it down. The fear and the facts always look smaller to me written on paper!!Replace negative thoughts with new thoughts and simple activities. I bless this inner mental work you will do for your future days of joy.

THE CHIPPED SEASHELL

I was in Jamaica one day on an early morning beach trip with my spiritual sons Gary and Shawn. I casually said to them I wanted a seashell with the coil shape in the center. Only because I saw one on display at our breakfast table as we ate our morning meal. So my simple wish must have gone deep into the heart of my son Shawn as he heard me mention the seashell I desired. Shawn had no money and lives in a very poor community. Shawn daily has to have faith to get even his basic needs for food met. His faith amazes me because Shawn truly trusts God to supply the things that he needs from day to day.

I watched him later swimming in the ocean so freely with no fear. Then he began to dive deep and stay under longer .Unknown to me he was using his faith under the water to search for the seashell I wanted! Shawn's faith was about to teach us all a deeper lesson as he was searching for the shell. He later popped up out of the ocean; his face was all drenched with water. He started running towards the sandy beach where I was sitting. With his big bright smile and Jamaican accent Shawn yells out with joy "Mommy catch dis I find de shell fa you! " He tossed it over to me with his child like faith still beaming all over his face.

I was so surprised and began to examine my new seashell found by my son just for me. Wow it was exactly what I wanted and wished for just a few hours ago. I then saw it had a small chip just one little piece missing on the back of the seashell and it was obvious that something had crushed it in one spot. I thought how did this happen? Was it done by a person's foot, did a bigger shell push it from the oceans current, or was it from a boat motor? We will never know the exact reason for the chip on the seashell but, the amazing thing was the seashell was still whole. The shell was still as God had designed it with its beautiful delicate coiled center and it was still intact enough to be recognized as a coiled seashell. The shell was still in the Jamaican waters with all the other shells and it still got "chosen". So the lesson is this: no matter what pain, chips, hurts or abuse that comes to our life we can be whole. We are still created as God designed us, we are whole, beautiful and we too are chosen. Today that seashell is like a valuable collector's item to me. I have it on display in my home on my office desk. It reminds me to have faith and when I see that seashell I always think chipped but not broken.

GOD'S CLEANSING RAIN

There are some hurts that appear to be so big; you wonder how can I ever overcome what I feel or heal from this inner sadness?

Well, I want to share a story of how amazing God's cleansing power is and he can wash away things that 10 years of counseling can't cure. Nothing is over night but with God's help all things are possible. God's healing will come in ways you never expect, but when it comes it is exact and perfect.

On the day my divorce was final, I was alone in Jamaica at a spa that's located in the mountains. It was my day of official freedom. I intentionally picked a place to be alone and peacefully transition into a place of wholeness free from abusive words. I had my spa package all scheduled but little did I know the blessing I was about to experience in my spirit.

I had a salt and glow body scrub; with hydro jet therapy. After the body scrub they release hydro jets on you and they step out of the room. I am on the spa treatment table no shower cap. Here comes the warm water. As the water began to flow I felt like I was alone in the rain with God. The water was on my body my face my hair and I felt like every hurtful thing I experience in my life was being rinsed off me, and the hydro jet water was more powerful than the pain in my heart. Happy tears began to flow from my eyes and I could feel the influence and connection to my former spouse leaving. The more I felt the connection leaving the water seemed to have the power of God in it. I'm telling you I really felt I was alone with God in a cleansing rain. I began to whisper wash away every pain and make me strong and whole Lord. When the water stopped I could hear the water going into the drains on the floor of the spa room. I thought YES, I'm free the past is over and I can start my new wonderful life alone.

I had instructed my lawyer to call my cell phone the moment the divorce had been filed with the court. When I checked my voice mail, the time of call came during the time I was under the hydro jet. The real place of healing was the intentional mindset I had to move on. So the natural water experience was only a manifestation of the deep intentions inside of me to heal. God in his kindness just allowed me to feel naturally what was already occurring in my inner thoughts. I was out of the darkness in God's light and then came the cleansing. I chose to forgive and let go of the past to experience the cleansing God had for my life. The deeper you forgive, the deeper the healing you receive will be. When you forgive look at it as sowing a seed to get a harvest of abundant healing.

I have experienced healing in ways I can't explain no matter how hard I try. The step by step process to healing is at times painful but the results are worth it. I feel as you advance don't look back, don't go back, and just keep going forward. Every day gets better and every year you will become stronger. The smile on your face will be so genuine because it comes from your inner undisturbed peace. There will be no person or event that can take it from you! The healing of your life is something you will work to obtain and be protective of this hard earned blessing .Healing comes from God and he can fix anything with time. Don't ever think you can't be healed or emotional hurts are too difficult to heal. You decide what will be healed NOBODY controls that, only you control that desire!! So say what you want to be cleansed and rinsed away from your life.

DECEPTION

In life we all need and desire meaningful connections with other humans. We want true friends around us and the genuine soul mate of our dreams. The journey of finding honest individuals will have many twist and turns. I am sure you will be disappointed at times and there is a strong chance you will interact with a person who is full of deception. My goal today is to help you relax and not worry, that others will hurt or trick you.

So, before I move on let's remember what deception is. Deception is merely a person making you think something that is not actually true. This individual starts out meaning no harm to you and in some perplexing way you really do interact with a part of the person that is good. However, in some twisted bizarre way this good person you are interacting with is only a small fraction of who they really are.

Now, I want the exciting opportunity to teach you why you should never fear this encounter of deception. When you realize where this deceiving behavior comes from and why it emanates from another person, you will be free from the fear of deception. Keep reading to discover how to forever be free from the deceptive manifestation a person presents to you.

Deception is crafted from an evil force that enters into the "weak" thoughts of another person. The key point is weakness is the breeding ground for deception to grow. A deceptive thought enters into their "weak" mind in a small dose then it grows from a little thought into a huge manifestation of deception. The person who was good now gets corrupted by this evil venom and becomes a carrier of deception. It's like they are a carrier of a disease! It's born from weakness so it has no true power against you.

This is why I always say, a person cannot harm me with their deception because in truth they will deceive their own self. They deceive their life and loose the wonderful opportunity to grow in good God connected relationships. Have you ever caught a person in a little white lie and thought what a waste of time?!! Remember, they wasted their time not yours! Now you know that they are deceptive, and now you can calmly press on in life without them.

If you have been deceived by others forgive them, and count it all as joy because you never have to give them another thought. This deceptive behavior is fruitless and a clear indication that they are weak. Please don't cry or feel embarrassed if you got deceived because you really have been blessed. Blessed that they have now revealed to you the authentic person that they really are, not the person they tried to make you think they were. It's time to smile and give thanks to the Most High God for this manifestation of deception. Add this to your strong thoughts and say it out loud when you are fearful....say this: _____ you can't deceive me._____ you are deceiving your own life may God take care of you. Now, release them into God's care. He can handle them better than you. God loves them more than you ever could. Remember, you are not rejected you are protected from evil.

LIE VISION

This is a phrase I started using to describe the negative force that will come to your thoughts. As you navigate on this new healing journey your mind is a powerful component for your healing. A television is a square flat screen device displaying pictures, movies, commercials and audio sound.

A lie vision is similar but it's a lie that comes to your inner thoughts first. Then the lie creates a pictorial vision and story line deep in your mind. These lies are lethal, strong, and most often they are accompanied with a low volume sound in your thoughts. That sound gets louder the longer you listen because it come from a very evil dark force and that evil force desperately needs your mind to work against you. I want to write about this and deal with this very quickly to help you heal.

As I mentioned earlier these lies most often take on a visual picture in your mind. You have to cut the lie vision off quickly. In other words, change the channel and turn the lie vision off in the same way you turn a TV off! If you don't turn the lie off you will begin to think about it, speak about it, and then you believe it. Oh, and it will make you cry like watching a sad movie!!

Ok I will confess sometimes I spoke about the lie vision and wow it's was so sad it would actually make tears come to my eyes. I realized I didn't like the tears and sadness that came with the lie visions. So I stop saying the lie or thinking about the lie vision. Amazing enough controlling the negative lie is really like changing the channel on a TV and the negative lie vision evaporates.

Poof the lie vision is then gone into thin air and you are back to your normal happy self. The lie vision needs a mind to rest in to live and grow. Don't allow your mind to every be a dwelling place for these awful lie visions! My Pastors wife, Sandie Chapman taught me this: we don't quote the devils thoughts we quote God's goodness. So, when we talk and I speak a fearful thought, she will stop me. She will then say, "Felicia don't quote the devil don't lift up his thoughts, you quote what God says about you." She taught me I give faith to what I say. That simple truth was a game changer as I healed. The teachers you need on this healing journey will come because God will send them to you. Some moments God will just come into your mind with new clear instructions therefore; be free of bitterness so you can hear the detailed instructions.

Today I can sense a lie vision very quickly. I now laugh when I hear a lie vision come to my thoughts. I will actually think and speak the exact opposite of what the thought is. Yes I let out a roaring laugh from a place deep in me! What a joyful feeling it is while laughing at a lie vision. I have moments when I stop with squinted eyes laughing!! This is the best because everything in you thinks the lie vision is now hilarious!! Just writing this makes me laugh and I hope a smile is on your face reading this. That smile on your face feels good right?? Now if there is a lie vision that has been lurking in your thoughts start laughing about it.

As I said, I speak out loud the truth and the lie somehow will vanish. The lie knows it can't come live in my mind, my environment nor in my new inner mindsets of peace. Sometimes I will just say "No not today" and I am actually saying out loud NO I refuse to think that, I will share more on that later. Remember if it's a bad thought change the channel. Speak out over and over, "That is not the truth!!" Then say the truth is _____ (you fill in the blank).

Some lies will try to stay in your mind because of the negative words that were spoken over you. You have to break the cycle of those words. You now choose to remove the lie visions even from past words. Yes, you can!! Let me teach you the facts and key points. Abusive people can't take responsibility for their actions. When they are rude they will tell you it's your fault. It sounds something like this, "If you stayed quiet you wouldn't get your feelings hurt." You have to say the truth to your own mind. It sounds like this; "He is rude and has poor self control and that's not my fault that he has a weakness." If you were made to feel you can't survive on your own, that's a lie. The truth sounds like this; "I am wise and an excellent manager of my money." In my singleness I have every provision provided, I've never had a bounced check and I have a very high credit score. So don't listen to the lies, create new visions of what you want your life to look like.

If this is difficult get a dear friend or family member to help you say loving truthful statements about your life. You would never watch a TV show you don't like so don't listen to a negative lie vision …

REMOVED FROM THE GRIP OF EVIL

One Saturday morning I went out for my latte and reading time. It's something I have as a weekend ritual to feed my spirit, be out among the living and avoid the poor me I'm alone trap.

Yes, I decided how I will think and what comes in my mind to be a part of my life. My Saturday morning ritual is so powerful because I set the time aside for me to relax. I actual look forward to the time as it brings a positive vibe to start my weekend. I gather my Bible, magazines, IPod, dress cute and start my weekend with joy. While out on a Saturday I read Palms 97 and to my surprise I saw a powerful truth on God's view of removing us from evil.

I think it is imperative that you clearly understand when something is evil or a person's actions are evil and toxic. I will be abundantly clear, if a person displays any type of abusive behavior that is extremely evil and manipulative. The abusive evil behavior can manifest verbally, physical, mental or sexually. I have never categorized one form of abuse as worse than the other because they are all EVIL and WRONG. We should never tolerate any form of abuse!! Okay now that we got that squared away let's see what God revealed to me that day in Psalms 97.

Psalms 97 reminds us that God is over all the earth, when we love God we don't like evil, God guards our life, and delivers us from the hand of the wicked. Light will shine on you again, and joy will be in your healed upright heart. God is higher and smarter than any person you will ever meet. God gives every person a purpose and that purpose is not to be dominated or abuse.

"For you, Lord are the Most High over all the earth; you are exalted far above all God's. Let those who love the Lord hate evil, for He guards the lives of his faithful ones and delivers them from the hand of the wicked. Light shines on the righteous and joy on the upright in heart. Rejoice in the Lord, you who are righteous, and praise his holy name." Psalms 97:9-12

Take refuge in God that he has delivered you from abusive hands or words. Praise God for the days of peace that are ahead for you. May God's refreshing rain come and began cleansing away all the evil that was around you. I feel it for you, it's about to rain!! Father I'm asking, "Wash and cleanse the thoughts of the one who reads this today. Amen"

WHAT IS GOD SAYING TO YOU?

The most important voice in my life is God's voice. I care about the thoughts of God and His spiritual guidance above any other opinions. When we are guided by our emotions, or the expectations of others we are sure to pick the wrong path. God's words in the scripture become a map to guide us in total confidence. Scripture reading evokes a quiet place of complete solace inside of me, and I experience increased strength from God. I have left space for you to list the impressions God desires to place in your spirit. Now, you can listen to God alone. What is God saying to you?

_____

_____

_____

_____

_____

_____

_____

_____

_____

_____

_____

_____

_____

_____

_____

_____

_____

_____

_____

WHAT IS GOD SAYING TO YOU?

_____

_____

_____

_____

_____

_____

_____

_____

_____

_____

_____

_____

_____

_____

_____

_____

_____

_____

_____

_____

_____

_____

_____

_____

_____

_____

_____

_____

No NOT TODAY!

In life we can decide what will accomplish on any given day. We have the opportunity to do good, do evil, procrastinate or reach our goals. Goals are looked at as short term or long term goals. There are some days you have various task that fit into the category of the short term goals. This can be very beneficial and rewarding because you are in motion. This motion causes a feeling of achievement and a positive vibe is all around you. Now in this positive mindset it will give you the momentum needed to reach long term goals. Your mind is like a power tool to build what you think and speak into being.

So, now you must understand how to use your mind as a power tool when you come upon a road block in your thoughts. This is when you say the power statement, "NO. NOT TODAY." You are refusing negative vibes that the mental road block is starting to create. Don't let the road block stop the momentum you achieved from your short term goals. I would like to suggest that you take a healthy pause. A healthy pause is needed to allow your emotions time to adjust. This is a moment that you can again decide how you will handle your day or life's unwanted disappointments. Sometimes the road block is designed to test you and when you handled it in a healthy pause you can still feel a sense of achievement. So, in the healthy pause feel free to still say, "NO not today." These words will give healing and strength to you. Now, you are saying in moment of difficulty. "No. I will not crumble in my disappointment." I get a kick out of saying to negative forces, "No. Today is not the day for this." "No. I am not going to think like that." I am speaking with power back to that negative force a strong, NO. We all have patterns of thoughts and behavior when a trial comes our way. Find your weak areas and get ready to say no to those thought patterns of fear and defeat. So your goal achieving momentum continues with a new spin on it to make you even stronger. These are 3 simple but powerful words "No. Not today."

LOVE BEING SINGLE

I know the thought of being single frightens most women. Our society puts great emphasis on romantic dates, holidays for couples, romantic get always, receiving gifts and most of all the engagement ring. The mere thought of that special person arriving in your life brings happy thoughts, a peaceful smile and a list of things you long to share with that person.

We must avoid the mental traps of having negative thoughts about our single status. Remember don't allow lie visions to come into your thoughts. The lie visions will be the following thoughts: fear of growing old alone or the deception that you are unwanted, not pretty, or you are not good enough. Please change the channel and never think that way about your life. You should begin to speak the truth about who you really are in your single status.

I want to share the secret of how to release the deep truth about yourself and I want you to say it daily until you believe it. Speaking these words will open up a deeper truth about the real person of value God has created you to be. The single person you see when you look in a mirror, that person is a work of art and now it's time to release that work of art to the world.. Please say the phrases exactly as its written divinely inspired from God's spirit. Say the following words daily: I am so pretty inside, I make wise choices, I am ready to know the purpose God created me, I am at peace, I look great from every angle, I am so fun to be around, I refuse fearful thoughts, I have a calm mind , I don't think anxious filled thoughts because those thoughts are not from God, I have great discernment, I follow right paths filled with light for my life and I remove myself from dark or negative issues/people.

If you struggle to say or believe theses statement it may signal areas you need to allow God to strengthen inside of you. If you find these words fit you exactly move ahead and enjoy the path that is before you. Until that person arrives love being single. When you love being single it allows the fullness of that season to flourish and you are able to enjoy each moment of your day.

When I wake up alone I love the quite solace I feel inside of my heart and that quiet solace is even in the air I breathe. I began to feel it was God's way of healing me from the past hurts and harsh words I use to hear. I speak to God in this peaceful morning air or in the quite of night time. I finally came to a place where I could say, "I trust your plan God." I am able to say, "Lord if you want me here alone with you so be it." I have learned that God will never withhold good from me. I use to read that in the scripture now I know the truth of those words. God never bring about events/people that will harm you or hinder His planned purpose for your life.

Musical Quiet Zone

Make time for the power of music in your home environment and plan for this to be done frequently. I find that piano instrumental music makes me feel extremely peaceful. It makes my home feel calm and restful while I am playing music. I began to understand that the music really gets inside me therefore; carefully pick what you listen to. Because the right music will make negative forces or thoughts become quiet. You are being reprogrammed so don't listen to sad love songs or the baby I want you back songs. Instrumental music or music with positive lyrics becomes very important as you heal.

For anxiety reduction I want to teach you a simple tip that's better than valium. Put your hand on your upper abdominal area and you need to inhale slowly and focus on making your stomach move your had out. Then slowly exhale and notice you hand moving back down. Do this 10 times and be aware of the air coming in and out of your body. What this will do is make you body send a signal to slow your heart rate and it will bring a calming effect. Now you can think clearly and continue your day or have a restful sleep. Also any paperwork or decision making forms are to be kept in your office or sitting area. Never bring it to your bedroom because your bedroom is for rest, sleep and peaceful thoughts. Honor your life with that gift and your bedroom becomes a positive place free of distressing energy.

My favorite CDs for you listening pleasure.

- Grace Williams (Heavens Rain and Take me away)
- John Fluker (The Sound of Peace)
- Paul Cardall (Faithful)
- Dan Gibson (Asian Spa) great for a bath with candles

CAPPUCCINO MOMENT

If you enjoy coffee today's message will really be an eye opener! Remember I shared I have a coffee shop I go to every week, and I enjoy the relaxed carefree environment. People are reading, on their computer or chatting with friends over warm aromatic cups of coffee. They even serve hot herbal teas, little biscuits, sandwiches and Belgium waffles.

I make this my Cappuccino moment alone and I treat myself to this moment to unwind. I feel peaceful and enjoy a moment I don't have to cook a meal.

Recently I had a friend share her sad feelings that her boyfriend didn't like taking her for coffee and he hated paying for her coffee and he felt she should just brew it at home.

I watched her eyes light up as she explained why she loved going to grab a coffee out even if it cost 4-5 dollars. She didn't have to explain it to me because I already knew it just makes her happy. I continued to listen to her explain her love of coffee and watching her big smile and her eyes filled with delight. This relationship with her boyfriend was over and there were several other rude behaviors he had displayed to her. I finally said to her, "I know the exact reason why he hated buying you the coffee or you even having a moment to get that cup of cappuccino." So now, I will share the explanation I told her about his behavior .....

He clearly saw that coffee makes her happy and peaceful deep inside. He hated that something so simple could evoke this deep happiness inside of her, and caused her to display that warm beautiful smile she has. When a person is mentally healthy they get joy from seeing you happy. They love sharing the simple joys of life with you. To be abundantly clear abusive people are manipulative, self centered, and want to control everything. If they find out something makes YOU happy they are coming after it. Abusive people are very weak minded fearful people, they act pushy and loud but inside they are hurting sad people. Somewhere in their childhood somebody hurt them, they carry a painful secret and now they live life hurting others. They know exactly what they are doing when they hurt you but, their pain is so deep they don't know how to be freed from their inner darkness. This darkness glooms over them like a plague in a dry desert. The words that they speak come from this gloomy dark place, which is why their words are heavy and hurtful. So now they are a full grown adult being a mean bully. Attempting to manipulate you and denying you of the joyful simple pleasures of life. Unfortunately this behavior doesn't stop at the denial of a cup of cappuccino. This behavior drifts slowly and deeply to every move you make, every desire and decision about your entire life.

This is the dark/negative force that you must remove yourself from. Seek clear paths of healing and happiness. I hope you will have many cappuccino moments and inner reflections to stay emotionally happy. Oh guess what? My friend has agreed to go with me to my favorite coffee shop. I will show her how to make her own cappuccino moment.

BE CAREFUL WHAT YOUR LITTLE EARS HEAR

I find it extremely amazing that our inner ear is so small but designed by God to hear sounds and the inner ear even controls our balance. So, we have the outer ear, and the middle ear that protects our inner ear. The words we hear go to the small inner ear. We hear a vast array of informative facts each moment of the day. We can hear a train before we see it. We can't see the wind, but we hear the wind blow. We hear the car horns blow to warn us of danger. As nurses, we hear medical training to care for the sick. We hear our phone voice mail, in crowded room. We can even hear announcements in a large airport that our gate number has changed. The same small inner ear can listen to the delicate sound of piano music. This inner ear can also hear kind words of love from a supportive loving relationship. So, this small inner ear translates vital information that determines our daily actions and helps us bond to another person to share a loving relationship.

So what are the effects when that same small inner ear begins to frequently hear harsh, rude verbal language? If you daily hear language that is filled with profanity, unsupportive, controlling, and insulting words that is not healthy. I think the inner ear can't properly interrupt this information as normal behavior to apply to our daily task. I think the little inner ear hears this awful language and signals to your emotions something is wrong. Your brain begins to translate the words and gives you a warning signal that you are in danger. When you hear the train coming, you know to get off the train track. You don't see the train but you hear it. You hear the bell ringing. The bar begins to lower at the rail road crossing track. You don't lay on the track or drive through the black and white bar at the rail road crossing; you stop in your vehicle. So, when your little ears hear the sounds of abusive and insulting words don't lay there. Don't keep going back to that person for love. Don't stay in that home environment you are in danger!

If you tolerate any rude harsh profanity filled words the following can occur: you will diminish the instinctive natural warning signal that comes to your mind and your thoughts will change to think this is normal. Hearing abusive words daily can harm your human emotions. You will feel crushed, drained and shattered emotionally. My God would never create your inner ear to hear or to translate these destructive words as normal. Nor should you life function from this type of hideous cruel information. Be careful what you let your little ears hear…Stay wise and keep a balance life to heal.

MAKING A POT OF SIMMERING CHILI

"Better a dry crust with peace and quiet than a house full of feasting and strife." Proverbs 17:1 NIV

The smell of good, fresh, and delicious food simmering in your home is a must. Cooking can be relaxing especially when it's just a few ingredients. Most of us are so busy with a full schedule and getting food from a fast food window can become a rut. Eating out is also very expensive. You may find that cooking in will really help your budget. Also left over's can become useful for lunches. For example left over roasted chicken can become a sandwich loaded with veggies or become a roasted chicken salad with Asian dressing .A big pot of chili can be served with a dinner roll or used as toping for a loaded baked potato.

You are on a new path of loving yourself in every area. In the scriptures Psalms 103 reveals a healthy tip. In Psalms 103 verse 6 it alerts us that when our mouth is satisfied with good things our youth will be renewed. So, healthy food renews our body and keeps us youthful. Cooking rules, as you cook no worries, no tears, and play some nice music. The goal is for you to find joy again in simple activities even if you are alone.

Yummy Chili Ingredients (Serves 4 people)

1 Onion diced

1 TBS olive oil

1 Pack ground Turkey

1/2 TBS red pepper flakes

1/2 TBS black pepper

1/2 TBS chili powder

1 Tsp Jamaican Scotch Bonnet pepper sauce

1/2 TBS salt

2 sprigs fresh thyme

1/2 Packet chili seasoning

1 20 oz can Peeled whole tomatoes

1 8oz can tomato puree

16 oz can Red Kidney beans (Rinse and drain beans)

In a large pot sauté the onions in the olive oil until transparent. Then add in the turkey, when the meat turns brown add all dry spices listed above except the thyme. (Stir and mix in the dry spices well). Cook this on med heat for about 5 min. Now dice the tomatoes into large chunks add in the tomatoes and the liquid from the can. Add in the tomato puree along with 1/2 can of water to rinse the tomato puree can. Now add the Kidney beans that were rinsed and drained. Stir well and allow to simmer for about 30 min may add additional water if needed. Add salt and pepper to your taste. Turn heat off. Insert the 2 sprigs of thyme. Leave covered and remove the thyme sprig before serving. I like cooking this early in the day on Saturday for an evening meal.

Intentional Actions

Most often the word intentional makes you think something negative happened. Our mind quickly thinks that if a person did something intentional surely it was done on purpose and has brought discomfort to others. Today we will look at the word intentional from a positive perspective.

Intentional definition: done in a way that is planned or intended; Deliberate and done by design.

God gave me a desire to live my days with intentional actions. If we look at the meaning of intentional actions: means living and doing things with purpose in mind.

After a loss or disappointment in our life, we have to make intentional plans to recover. I am very persistent to see good outcomes for my personal life, and I realize I am the only one who can reach the purpose God has planned for my life. I wake up with the intention to have the following: A peaceful day, read to enhance knowledge, refuse to worry, speak positive about my life, treasure inner contentment, dismiss toxic behaviors, accomplish today's tasks, manage my finances, give away lots of smiles, find humor in difficult moments, and encourage others. These are my intentional behaviors, because they make me successful in all areas of my life. I also enjoy being around the peaceful energy God has placed inside of me, and it radiates from my life into my personal environment. Stand up, wipe away your tears, make new plans, and let your life be filled with intentional actions.

You can do whatever you dream for each day. You are in the driver's seat and God is the navigator. He is showing you the mental things to delete and when to do a reset. Connect into God's designed plans for your life. Whatever you do, do it with great intentions.

Be Wise and know God's will

"Be ye not unwise but understanding what the will of the Lord is. Don't act thoughtlessly, but try to find out and do whatever the Lord wants you to." Ephesians 5:17 (KJV)

If you are being abused in any manner you must get out safely and don't go back. Your emotions and fear of being alone may make you waiver. Some women initially struggle with thoughts like should I stay; should I leave, and maybe this can get okay? When I got out I immediately felt so safe and calm that I never desired to go back. For my life, I trusted my inner gut. Going back into the relationship didn't feel like a safe or healthy option, for me.

Most studies show that abusive behaviors in a person usually will NOT stop. This can be difficult to hear because we want to save the marriage covenant or dating relationship. In addition to this, most people didn't marry an abusive spouse. There are cycles of calming but the rude violent behavior usually returns. This behavior usually intensifies and becomes more frequent.

Getting out to a safe place to live helps protect your life and allows the process for your emotional healing to start. Upon leaving I was very tired and needed to start the refreshing of my healing. A quiet room free of abusive language felt like an oasis in the dessert to me.

Years later, I then began to teach others that you don't focus on fixing domestic violence but you need to first protect yourself from violence. Forgiveness is done by forgiving the abuser for the wrong and rude actions done to you. You will notice even in my writing I address protection FIRST then the next goal is FORGIVENESS. As a Christian I would hear of a few cases where women went back and they were okay. I just speak caution and encourage you to get clear direction from God for your life. Every situation is different so be prayerful and look at the specific details of your situation.

I have a dear Jamaican pastor who gave me these wise words, "Felicia none of us can tell you to go back; you must be safe. Going back home will be between you and God."

Note: I did not go back. I did everything possible to remove my life and finances away from my former spouse. I was guided by God to see, I could not heal or recover in an abusive atmosphere. God gave me common sense. My thoughts could not be dominated by another person. I took the path of leaving for healing; clearly and wisely directed by God.

PHYSICAL AND FINANCIAL STABILITY

Ask yourself; am I in a safe place and protecting my money to survive? Organizing practical matters for day to day living will bring security to you as you heal. This is very crucial because abusive relationships can deplete feelings of stability from your life. Each person will be in a different place. But pull from these handy tips to assist you in becoming independent and stable. You need to gain back feelings of stability, then you can focus deeper on your inner healing. Apart of being an independent woman is having an organized life. As an independent woman, you must find a place of physical and emotional stability. Just because you are a married woman, does not mean you are not independent; you still have to think for yourself. We all know that when you get married, two shall become one. In other words, what you bring to the table should not get lost or trampled. You have a voice and you can think for yourself; and your wisdom should be respected. The voice God gave you was stolen. You have to reclaim your voice and the ability to hear the voice of God. This is a major step to move ahead in allowing yourself the opportunity to now make wise and sound decisions to live the peaceful life you deserve. Use the check list below to organize your needs. Add new numbers to your cell phone for emergency, business and quick reference. Let me take a moment to explain to you why this check list is extremely important for your healing journey.

1. Consider changing your home and cell number to unpublished numbers. Doing this was a major moment of extreme peace and empowerment for me. Changing the phone numbers also made a bold statement in MY own heart. The abusive language was over and I no longer had to hear one word of profanity, ever again. Abusive people need to see the boundaries and understand; you will not be manipulated or have a war of words. Change the number even if you had it for 20 years. You can give out new phone numbers to the people who matter most and those who will protect you as you heal.
2. Turn off the answering machine until you get your private unlisted phone number. Never allow the abuse to continue via phone conversations, text messaging, fax, or on an answering machine. You can't reason with an abusive person so cut the ties. When you cut these ties it's a pivotal moment of your healing. You might be accused of being rude or unfriendly but it's not the case. You are simply done with the abuse and respect yourself enough to set boundaries.
3. Child care needs consider giving a family or friend's number for relaying messages. Spare your home life from words of abuse or negative voice mail. Keep a peaceful environment. To have peace in your new home and promote a restful environment.
4. Open private bank accounts: checking/savings with check protection. Add bank phone number to your cell.
5. Alert your financial advisor or 401 program consultants that only you are to indorse changes.
6. Hire and find your own lawyers. Don't use people who you both knew.
7. File taxes separate even during the separation time.
8. Join AAA for auto emergency tire changes or towing.
9. Find a new person to do your auto repairs.
10. Find a local tire repair shop.

11. Do a PO Box for your mail.
12. Shop at different super markets / drug store.
13. Have your car washed at the Brushless drive through places.
14. Don't eat at your old spots; find new places this is fun!
15. Don't take advice from people that have bitterness or selfishness connected to it.
16. NEVER have the abusive person in your new dwelling. If you have to meet, do the meeting in an open place with others. (no sex tell you why later)

You will find that these steps and tips above will strengthen your life. You are the only one who can make the transitions needed. When you want healing you will take the necessary steps to remove the negative energy from around you. Remember, you are stabilizing your life and that is your only focus. You cannot organize the life of another adult. Avoid all conversations, which seek to make you responsible for their financial resources and well being. You are not the ATM or their counselor. You are not available to listen to any issues or needed items. You are in healing mode.

I think you are about to start feeling the rain on your face!! Please be safe, be prayerful for guidance, and find your own stability.

CLIMB THE LADDER

It has been said over and over that life is about perspective. When you have been in an abusive relationship, the painful feelings can shape how you view and feel about life. Sometimes, we have been so low, so crushed or hurt we risk seeing life through eyes of pain. We must climb out of that place to see the beauty of life and the beauty from other humans.

Recently, I needed to replace a light bulb on my front porch and the step stool I had was not taking me high enough to reach it; and I was unable to see the bulb wattage. I went to a local store to purchase a ladder. I actually stood up on two different ladders to see which ladder had the height; I thought would reach the light bulb.

While at the store, I was sharing my excitement of my new peaceful home with a lady working at the store. I also shared I was single, whole and deeply healed from the verbal abuse from my past. The lady became teary eyed and said, "If I ever get out of my marriage I will never marry again because I hate men." My heart filled with compassion for her because I knew she needed a spiritual ladder to see this differently and I knew she was being abused in her home. I said, "No you don't hate men. You hate the abusive spirit that comes from your spouse." I shared with her to forgive him and seek a way to find protection from the abusive partner she was living with.

I had already been climbing a ladder spiritually to have this restored perspective about marriage and men. While looking for a ladder in the store, I helped another human soul climb a ladder of healing. My spirit has no bitterness; no fear of men or fear marriage if that's God's plan. The depth of God's healing and restoration inside of me brings me abundant peace. My emotional healing flows out to others. When I see a hurting soul the healing in me spills over towards their heart. I would like to see them restored as well.

When I got home I did change that light bulb easily with my new ladder. The higher ladder gave me a higher perspective, it was easy to reach and see what to do in changing a simple light bulb. Without climbing the ladder, I was helpless in mastering the simple task.

What is it that you desire to see today from a higher perspective? Come climb the ladder and get the better perspective, you desire. God passionately desires to give you new vision; emotional healing and healthy perspectives about who you are to the world. It looks good up here. Come on. Climb up!!

WHO'S GOING TO LOVE ME?

As a human we give love to others. We all have the desire to be loved and cared for in return. I think it's normal. After all, we were loved by our parents or guardians. Most of us grew up feeling the care of our parents; having our meals prepared, and help from our family. As we grow older we realize there are different types of love. A normal maturing person wants love. Our hearts and human emotions continue to expand in the quest for love.

Leaving an abusive relationship takes a great amount of strength; especially when you did feel loved at one time by that person. The new path you face alone is uncertain. You find yourself saying, "Who's going to love me now?" It is a deep concern to most women. It can bring absolute fear when you think about it. "Who's going to love me?" This is a power packed question. When we think about it, it can mean something different to all of us. You know what makes you feel loved. We all know the little things that communicate love in our brain.

My goal with today's reading is to make you remember what love is. I want to help you remove the fear that you will never be loved again. I had that fear. It's a fear that will send your mind into a downward spiral of sadness; if you think on it too long. I notice when I thought about not being loved ever again by a man; it would bring a gloomy darkness over my mind. It would consume the atmosphere to the point, I felt mentally paralyzed. After several episodes of that I made a deal with my own brain to not think of it, ever again. It took strength to leave an abusive relationship. It took an equal amount of strength to refuse, thinking about who's going to love me now.

The first step of freeing my mind from the fear of not being loved- was to identify what is love? The bible says, God will give us the desires of our heart. I have my list and the core qualities on that list include the following themes: respect, honesty, gentleness, a lover of God's Holy Word and a person who presence radiates goodness. In truth I just gave you words that describe who I am at the core of my own heart.

But the word clearly tells us what love is: "love is patient, love is kind. It does not envy, it does not boast, it is not proud. It does not dishonor others, it is not self-seeking, it is not easily angered, it keeps no record of wrongs. Love does not delight in evil but rejoices with the truth. It always protects, always trusts, always hopes, always preserves. Love never fails." 1 Corinthians 13:4-8 (NIV)

First of all this narrows the search of love very quickly and brings you to a place of patience. Secondly, you continue to trust God's divine plan to add to your life what you deserve in His divine timing.

Another question you have to answer is: do I know how to love myself? A big sign of how much you love yourself is: to no longer allow harmful people to remain in your life. The first person that's going to love you now is YOU!! This powerful revelation needs several days and hours of deep reflection. You may have to read this section for the next three days. You will love you..

Remember, God's word say love is patient, kind, not easily angered, rejoices in the truth, bears all things, hopes all things and it never fails.

1. In this time be patient with the inner pain you feel.
2. Be kind to only think good thoughts about yourself.
3. Don't get angry when you disappoint yourself.
4. Rejoice in making sound decisions to be free from abuse.
5. Continue this healing journey
6. Think wise thoughts
7. Have hope for a beautiful life as you heal.

I can't answer the question of if you will be in a loving relationship with a soul mate. I can say you can love yourself and the purpose God has for your life. You will be amazed now, the healthy things you will do for your own healing. For the next 7 days write down the things you do daily to love yourself.

Examples

1. Refuse a negative phone call
2. Let go of a sad self pity thought
3. Put on a cute dress and paint your toe nails too
4. Get in some exercise time and buy a cute bottled water to sip on
5. Cook a healthy dinner for YOU set the table and light a candle
6. Buy yourself coffee at a nice coffee shop and read a book while there
7. Do a name fast (you don't say the abusers name for a week)
8. Buy a new vase for the fresh flowers you will frequently buy for yourself

I have listed a few examples above but, now go have the joy of witting your own actions of self love.

Activities to Nurture My Life

_____

_____

_____

_____

_____

_____

_____

_____

_____

_____

_____

_____

_____

_____

_____

_____

_____

_____

_____

_____

_____

_____

_____

_____

_____

_____

CHOCOLATE CAKE

Just the title of today's writing makes you want to read this right? Don't we all love moist chocolate cake? Chocolate cake in this message represents something we like. We have to be wise and honest about what we partake of in life. A lovely friend of mine had a problem. She wanted to push away factual parts of what was going on around her. I told her, "If you eat chocolate cake and wipe the crumbs and icing off the edge of your mouth; it doesn't mean you didn't eat the cake. The truth is you are only wiping off the obvious evidence from your face, but it doesn't mean you didn't eat the chocolate cake. No matter, how clean you wipe your mouth, you ate the chocolate cake. The truth is the chocolate cake is now inside of you. In addition to that, you can't just wipe the mental memory of your chocolate cake eating experience. We must think about our action before hand. Is it worth eating the chocolate cake? What I'm really saying is, be wise with what you consume. What God has for you is for you. You don't have to partake of things God has not planned for you. God gave Adam and Eve boundaries. The wrong path, wrong people, or wrong actions can feel and taste good just like the yummy delicious chocolate cake. We can swiftly wipe away cake crumbs but a series of wrong actions and wrong people around us cannot be merely whisked away in two seconds. Our wrong or ill timed actions will set into motion a series of events that alter who we are and what we truly believe. The right chocolate cake is the goodness that God has plan specifically and precisely for you to eat!!

What is the wrong chocolate cake you are partaking of today? Something that feels or seems good but upon deep self introspection you see it's a hindrance to your life or the true value of who you are.

"When a person sins they are drawn away by the lust in their own heart." James1:14

Here is a prayer I pray to help me not eat the wrong chocolate cake and I hope you can pray it for your life today. I actually pray it with my hand over my human heart. It's a simple gesture that shows God, I honestly desire to surrender anything wrong in my heart. My human plea during this prayer is so real. I without doubt believe that any evil known or unknown will leave my heart as I yield my mind and body to God.

God, I pray You would let me see things as You see them. Fill my heart with only what you desire for my life. Lord, may I not desire one thing or event that you have not planned for me. Fill my heart now with only Your will. Let even my human thoughts and desire reflect what You see and have plan for me. Lord, let me not worry about today or the future. Let my heart seek what You see as good for me. Now, Lord I thank You that You direct the traffic of what comes into my life or leaves out of my life. I thank You for the good expected hope and future You have plan just for me .Oh my Lord! You sit high and You look low seeing what I can't see or plan. I choose to trust You. I trust You and wait with peace and joy for your direction. Amen

LORD NAVIGATE MY MIND

When I hear the word navigate, I think of being lost and needing to get to a certain place safely. I also think of how wonderful GPS devices are to help us navigate to an unknown place. With a navigator we are free of the stress that we will get lost.

Upon ending a long term relationship, you can also feel lost. You are unsure of what's ahead. In your healing process feeling this way is very normal. You need to find a new way of living and thinking. I began to daily pray the following simple words... Lord navigate my thoughts.

I had to think new thoughts about me. I refused to think about the abusive controlling words that had been chanted at me. Now, on my own, I had to set up my home and finances for daily survival. I am now able to get up and think about what I want to do and the way I want to accomplish it. The basic right of every human is to have God direct them. Sure, you work together as a family, share ideals and desires with each other. However, your spirit and mind should never be dominated and ruled by another human.

God is the true navigator. When He leads you, He is gentle and guides you in a peaceful manner. Also in a marriage a good spouse will lead with the gentle loving manner of God. They will have a deep respect for the relationship. God will help you let go of the past pain and thoughts that trouble you. When you ask God to navigate your thoughts, He somehow organizes your thoughts to see the truth. You began to see that abusive people are hurting, insecure, weak, and fearful people. You will quickly learn to release their harmful words and think about them less and less. God, will navigate your mind to think in a healthy manner as you heal. The outcome of these healthy thoughts will bring inner comfort, positive and productive actions for your new life.

I love asking God, to navigate my thoughts and I find He will help me turn some thoughts off. If you go the wrong way with your GPS while driving your car, the voice will command you to turn around. There are days we need to stop going down certain mental paths. If not, we will have what I call a mental wreck. A mental wreck is where our thoughts will cause an emotional crash of doubts, tears, loneliness, and fear. As you are moving towards your place of healing, don't allow a mental wreck to stop your progress. Your thoughts can take you down a dark road with no street lights. Although, you are mentally lost, allow God, the Navigator to reroute your path.

I have worked long and hard to enjoy the positive outlook, I have on life now. I am very selective as to what I allow to stay in my thoughts. If a thought makes me teary eyed or have fear of the future, it gets tossed out. I mentally turn my thoughts away. I refuse it. God has taught me how to do this. I think about what I have, not about what I don't have. Also, I think about what I have gained, not about what I have lost.

I hope you will ask God to navigate your thoughts. Get back on a healthy mental path. When you begin to pray for God to navigate your thoughts, you will see amazing results.

You basically, begin to learn how God wants you to think. You will find yourself cutting thoughts off, turning around from old mindsets. You will have an increase of healthy mental thoughts. You will become protective of your thoughts to guard the healing you have already obtained. The hard work is done.

You are becoming a strong powerful person to give back to the world. You can give to the people who love you. God is navigating not only your thoughts but your entire life. What thoughts do you need to surrender to God's navigation? Please allow this powerful transformation to begin, today. You will find great mental progress. You will quickly surrender things more and more to the Navigator!! Don't waste any more time on the wrong mental paths and having mental wrecks. Just softly whisper the prayer. "Lord, navigate my thoughts."

The Transition

"You are getting ready to go into a deeper

transformation of your healing."

-Felicia Jamison

THE FEAR CYCLE

It has been said that fear can be beneficial to help us in a crisis or to be more observant. I personally don't like feelings of fear. I tend to not want that emotion on a high level inside of me. Fear is an unusual emotion when not dealt with. Other emotions come in and hide behind fear. I want to deal with the cycle of fear that makes a person handle disappointments poorly. In the dark shadow of fear you will make bad decisions.

In this cycle we will have the primary emotion of fear; then anxiety will try to creep in. Fear of rejection is the next part of this cycle. As a result, these various emotions will cloud your thinking and cause you to respond poorly to disappointments. The scripture says perfect love cast out fear. I never really knew what that meant. I thought perfect love was a person's actions. I now know that perfect love is God's love. There is not one human being that can ever be perfect in their love towards you. However; God's love towards you is perfect. God is perfect in how He loves you at every season of your life.

In my singleness, I watch God's divine guidance over small details of my life. I was on a personal vacation alone in Aruba; and God spoke so clearly to me. "Just me and you, Felicia. As your heavenly Father, I want to heal you."

After hearing God's voice, all fear started to fade and a peace began to fill my heart. I have a famous saying about God...When we do things on our own we rush it. BUT when God is doing something for you, He takes His time. You can trust that God is looking at details. You can't even imagine. He is in no rush, because He has a wonderful outcome designed just for you. So trust Him!!

SAYING *I LOVE YOU*

The three words every human soul longs to hear, I love you. The whisper of these three words, I love you can evoke an eruption of feelings. The feelings can range from joy, peace or tranquility. We long to hear it from our parents, spouse and friends. However, we have not heard it until we can hear it come from within ourselves. We need to love ourselves, first.

Life after abuse can leave you feeling very unloved and barren. This is a time where the true validation of who you are can only come from you. After leaving there were days I would be driving only to realize tears were rolling down my face. A deep sense of sadness would overtake me. I would realize I had not been loved as I should have been. The abusive harsh words and actions were not love.

In sad moments while alone, I found myself saying these words softly out loud, "Felicia I love you." It was me saying to myself, "I love you". I was saying the three famous words to my own soul. It became the most calm and peaceful words to my own soul. I felt like I was writing a script for a movie and I was in the starring role. I would say my lines over and over.

Felicia: I love you.
Felicia: I will take good care of you.
Felicia: I will buy you flowers.
Felicia: I will take you out to eat.
Felicia: I will rent a movie for you.
Felicia: I will buy you a new perfume.
Felicia: I will take you on vacation.

In the sincere love of my own well being, I not only said these things to myself, I did these things for myself. I did it with great joy. Why? I really love myself.
Don't be eager to fill your life with just any man or date just anybody. Have a high standard for a new spouse. He should be able to love you on the level similar to how you love yourself. In the bible it says, two shall become one flesh in a marriage. In a healthy union, each person should love the other as they love their own flesh. I pray you will let God, set up the plan and purpose. No matter what, be able to say, I love you to your own soul, today and always…

TRANQUIL MIND

The word tranquil mean: calmness, or a peaceful state of mind. There are two times of the day that I strongly feel this in my mind. I feel tranquility when I wake up; and when I lay down to sleep at night.

When you are worried, fearful or afraid, it is impossible to have feelings of tranquility. Peace cannot rest in your mind or your spirit when it's filled with fear. In my singleness, I began to feel a strong sense of inner peace and serenity. Some people love drama and speaking rude words. However, if you come in touch with true peace, it's a lovely addiction!! Having peace is like having money in the bank or getting a fabulous outfit!!

I made room in my mind for peace. The more I felt peace, the more I desired peace. Finding peace for yourself is so vital on your journey of healing. Upon finding this place of peace, you only allow or add things into your life which adds tranquility. When something begins to distress me, I began to analyze it. I quickly clear it out of my mind and seek God's direction to handle this distressing feeling. Sometimes, it could be a trigger of an old memory of pain. If this is the case, I allow myself to sort out the truth. In that very moment, I ask myself, "What is really going on?" This allows me to grown and not run away from the distress. I get clarity. I get stronger.

A tranquil mind gives you the ability to do the tasks that are before you. I gained strength from the peace, which came to rest in my mind. I began to see my goals. I also remembered activities I once enjoyed. With my peaceful mind, I read books. I had to continue my missions work in Jamaica. In this quiet place, sitting on a balcony, overlooking the ocean, I began to write the book you are currently reading.

Where will you put your energy today?? I pray you refuse to feel anxious. You need to make room for tranquility to enter your mind. Let the addiction of tranquility abundantly flow in your life. As you heal, enjoy the days of calm stillness. Never, fear a quiet room. In that quiet stillness, God is always there with you.

YOU ARE NOT LONELY YOU HAVE YOURSELF

~I once was lost but now I am found. Was blind but now I see~

As a survivor of domestic violence, I shared my story with a dear friend of mine. As a brilliant and extremely busy surgeon, I felt blessed, that he took the time to care about my life. When he found out, he cheered me on. He said to me, "Only a strong person can walk away from that life." From time to time, he would check on me as we pass each other in the hospital hallways. I said to him one day. "It's been three years and I am still alone." Dr. Weaver gave me one of his warm smiles and said. "You're not alone." "You have yourself!!" I never knew what a deep impact those words would have on me. My entire perspective began to change. I thought, "Hummmm I'm with ME." Wow! I began to think about the wonderful person I am. I am a wonderful friend, to my friends. I am humorous. I am kind. Then I thought, "You are not alone, Felicia. You are with an amazing human being, 24 hours a day." I share this story to make you think about how truly wonderful you are.

Abuse can shatter the perspective of who you are. I have heard women say, "In the abuse, I lost myself." It is vital not to start a new relationship. You need to be single and find out who you really are. As I said, you will see how amazing YOU are. In your time of singleness, you have to be careful of speaking negative or empty words. Don't speak words of doubt.

DON'T SAY, "I'm so lonely. I feel so alone." These are statements will bring dark, gloomy, sad, and lost feelings. I must confess, I said these things. I would feel like a lost child; sitting alone with salty, hot tears streaming down my face. I STOP saying it. I realize my emotions began to heal and new positive thoughts of my single life became easy. There was so much to explore. There was so much to rebuild. There was no time to feel self pity or loneliness. Now, I had energy to do anything, I wanted to do!

Today you are being given the gift of finding YOU. Finding yourself is a powerful gift. You must press ahead and explore all angles of who you are. I remember how much I loved music, ballet performances, art and reading great books. I can read till I fall asleep, because I love the power of written words. Words stir us to change and grow. Just mere printed letters on a page challenge us, enlighten us and make us feel warm and comforted.

Take a moment to remember who you really are. Think about all the wonderful kindness you give to others. You are not alone. You have yourself. Use your strength. The same kindness that you give to others, give it to yourself as well.

PACK YOU'RE ABOUT TO MOVE!

Have you ever had to pack for a move to a new location? You will find things and you wonder why you kept it so long. You also need to let go of items but it has a memory of happy times or a family member. As you see the mountain of items, you start to realize something has to get left behind.

Our life is constantly moving. We somehow don't pack and toss out things within us; things that should be left behind. There are even relationships we need to pack and release. When we move to another dwelling place; we pack nice, used, items and give it to Goodwill. Why do we do that? We do it because the item can be used by another person. The items are no longer needed in our home. There are some items you throw in a big black trash bag!! When I packed and moved to my new home that was my favorite thing. I put useless items in the black trash bag and down the trash chute it went. I don't have a memory of what all went in those black trash bags, but I can tell you I used a lot of them. Some of those black trash bags were heavy too. When I got in my new home it was so easy to unpack because I was very determined while packing not to bring useless items with me.

How determined are you to pack away or toss out painful thoughts and your fears? I say pack them away and toss them out as you are on this healing restorative journey. This step is not for the faint of heart, because old mindsets will want to stay with you. You are the only person who can pack them away in the black trash bag and toss it. Some things don't want to be put in that bag, because that thing is designed to stop you from being happy. I say just go on, put it in the black trash bag and down the trash chute it goes.

Pack, because you're moving to a new place in your own human heart and thoughts!! The useless thoughts are too heavy for you to carry. You can't move ahead with heavy distressing mental thoughts inside of you, as they will weigh you down. These thoughts must not be allowed in your future.

On my days of sadness I had to choose what I would think about and boldly tossed out thoughts that hindered my progress. So now it's your moment to pack away useless mental items and move in the light hearted peaceful life ahead of you. Make room for new thoughts, new plans and new adventures. This is the fun part of the journey, because you will see the vibrant happy person you were meant to be. You will now look in the mirror at your happy eyes that are filled with God's light. With these new insightful eyes you will clearly see how to move ahead.

Prayer for today: God please show me what to let go of and what useless memory to toss out. Show me the truth and how to move ahead today. Amen

PROVERBS CHAPTER 2

Today you need to get your bible and have it beside you as you prepare to read.

I am writing today about Proverbs Chapter 2, because it became a point of reference for me as I healed. I looked to this section of scripture directed by God. Teary eyed one morning I reached for my bible seeking peace for that day. I had no other place or person to reach out to. I only had my God. So I flipped a few pages in my bible and my eyes fell upon Proverbs Chapter 2.

As I began to read my heart was flooded with peace and a power from above. The Word of God gave me profound insight and eradicated fears from my heart. I actually felt it was a pivotal moment for me to continue the healing journey and to even finish writing this book. A new joy came over me, as I sat alone reading His Word. While reading I was very sure of God's ability to care for every part of my life. I also knew this was not a coincidence!

The concepts that blessed me in Proverbs Chapter 2 were the following: We should listen to God and cherish His words. Our ears should desire to listen to Him. We should cry out to Him when we need direction. When we seek God, He will grant us a lot of good common sense. As we are honest, He will protect our path. He will shield us from evil. We can understand what is wise, right or fair for us. His wisdom will keep evil from us and keep us from people who walk on dark paths.

So now go to your bible and read Proverbs Chapter 2 and pray over your life. Find His direction for the things that make you tearful or afraid. Directions for resolution of your greatest fear or pain are about to come upon you today. His peace will fill your heart and remove your fears. Go now to your quiet place with God and His solace for you in Proverbs Chapter 2.

RIGHT THING WRONG SEASON

From the time we were children there have been moments we all wanted something that was not good for us. We have wanted too much candy, didn't wear a jacket to school, wanted popcorn before dinner, played before doing homework or have gone out with friends who did not add to our goals. None of the above desires would kill us, but we wanted them at the wrong time or with the wrong friends.

As we become wise adults, it becomes even more important to avoid doing the right things in the wrong season. When we are in a season of healing, it's not the season to build a new relationship. God created us to have relationships; we clearly see God gave Adam his lovely Eve so he would NOT be alone. Relationships are designed by God, so they are a good thing. God was with me as I built my new home. It was a natural process to watch my house come from the foundation up. I learned how strong I was and how God was rebuilding me emotionally during this house building process. I could see my new emotional foundation was being formed alone and upon this new stronger emotional foundation God would help me rebuild a healthy life. When I saw this beautiful home emerge I wanted my life to mirror this home. I filled my home with peaceful colors and lovely furniture. My home helped me to realize that I only wanted peace around me and whoever comes into my life needs to bring 'that' peace with them.

My prayer for you is to know the season you are in and embrace it. Learn the lessons you need to learn for each season of your life. We can't rush away winter nor can we make spring come any sooner. As a natural season changes we enjoy the events of that season. I enjoy wearing winter coats and eating warm winter soups. I don't worry about spring and somehow the spring flowers emerge with their sweet scents without any effort from me. I don't try to have sweet summer fruits in the dead cold of winter. Summer is coming and the fruit of that season will be worth the wait.

Please endure patiently the season you are in. In each season learn everything God desires to teach you. This endurance will help you avoid reaching for the right thing in the wrong season.

I pray for the right things to come to you in the right moment and season. It will be like eating chicken chowder on a cold winter day; fresh cut flowers in spring or homemade ice cream with fresh summer berries. Enjoy your current season with no worries because your emotional season will change just as winter will change to spring in God's time.

CHANGE YOUR NAIL POLISH

Today is a light hearted message to make you simply smile. Yes, I want you to change the color of the polish on your toes! I want you to pick a color you never have worn in your entire life. Don't pick anything in a pink or red tone; if that's the colors you usually wear. This simple task is about change. Something that you have done one way can change no matter what it is. You will want to look at your old polish colors. You will have to push yourself to find a new color as you look at various polish colors. This will be so much fun for you.

As I was healing, I did this and found an electric light blue color. Once my pedicure was done and I looked down and saw my new color, I was in shock because it was dazzling! New! Electric, so cute and unique! This change was a spark that made me smile. The next time I got a minty green color. Then one day, I wanted nail art painted on my big toe nails only. The Asian man who gave me a pedicure said, "You want something special or a surprise?" I said, "Surprise me!!" He said in his lovely Asian accent…"No looking. No peeking till I finish." Well, when he was all done, I looked down and he had painted a daisy on each of my big toe nails. It looked like the art work of a five year old. He said ….."How you like it?" I said, "I LOVE it!!" I loved it because it looked like a five year old had painted it and it made me laugh soooo hard. I got home and would crack up laughing every time I looked down at the polish on my big toe nails. I kept the design for about two weeks. I laughed myself silly like a child, every morning when I looked down at my feet. So much pain was around me, but the nail art made me laugh.

Go out today and change your toe nail polish and smile. As you do it, let it be the moment you know even your current emotional pain can change too. I have chosen courage instead of self pity. The little outing for you to change your toe nail polish will teach you the wonderful power of choice. As you get your pedicure or get a friend to paint your toe nails think about what emotional changes you desire to make. May you find life's simple joys in all that you do. As long as you are alive find a moment to smile, it will heal you. The scriptures say a merry heart is like medicine.

SINGLE RED ROSE

When I separated myself from the abusive environment I was in, God began to reprogram my thoughts. He told me I was to present myself to others as a single woman not a divorced woman. God told me, you are now like a single red rose and full of beauty. God was really nice to do that for me. He began to paint a picture in my mind of how He saw me and how I was to see myself. God used His floral creation of a Rose to help me heal.

When I felt sad, I would think of how beautiful Roses smell. A smell like no other flower, very distinct, yet delicate.

Today, I share this concept with you to remind you that you too are a single Rose. You deserve to have daily; the happy emotions a Rose evokes. People get Roses and they smile, feel warm inside, cry happy tears and feel loved by the sender.

My new home has Rose shrubs that have single bloom Roses. They have that classic red Rose scent. It's a joy to go outside, feed them and cut a few to put in a vase for inside my home.

I look at them and feel so much joy to have a home again and even have fresh cut flowers from my yard. To look at them reminds me I am beautiful and valued by God and most of all I value myself. I value the life I am living in peace and quiet.

I feed my Roses every week and they flourish!! When I cut some to bring inside I love having one that is about to open. I can then watch it bloom over the next few days. Caring for the Roses reminds me how important feeding my spirit and mind positive things will make me flourish. I also know I am still blooming and becoming exactly who God desires me to be. So are you......

ABUSERS ARE NOT YOUR FRIEND

Proverbs 17:17 A friend loves at all times.

I am sharing on this topic not out of bitterness or unforgiveness, but to help others choose wise, simple paths for their future. Most women tend to be loving and nurturing beings. Once in a relationship, most women love the friendship factor that they have shared with a person. We have all been in friendships that ended. The person changed or moved and the season of that friendship ends. As the old adage says, some relationships are for a reason, a season or a lifetime. Then, there are friends that move to another city and we don't talk to them very often. However, in just one phone call or face to face reconnection the richness remains. It's their genuine love for you, that brings the richness of love to the surface quickly and it's like no time has been lost. I have a dear friend named Cathy in Jamaica; we only see each other a few times every year along with phone calls. When we have face to face moments on her veranda in Kingston, it's like no time has passed and I can't wait to have coffee with her and laugh. We make the best jokes about our own mistakes and disappointments. After my divorce, Cathy would say in her Jamaican accent "Felicia, de Lord will hold you now that you are alone." I didn't want to hear those words, because I was hurting and I wanted another soul mate. Her words were never meant to hurt me, even though it was painful to hear. Now, we can laugh about it together, I even like to imitate her Jamaican accent back to her and we laugh ourselves silly like two little girls. Now, that's a true friend. They cry when you cry, they laugh when you laugh and always tell you the truth.

When you share your love, laughter, resources, energy and supportive assistance with a spouse, the results should be their love comes back to you. I just live life like simple math 1+1=2 and 2+2=4. To me, love+giving=kindness not cursing, yelling, demanding or controlling another person's actions. Sure, we make requests or express our desires to people that we are friends with or love, but we should never make controlling demands.

My best friend Crystal has been in my life since 9th grade. In my days of sadness or weakness Crystal would never let me say negative things. Crystal would say "Felicia, I can't let you say that over your life." "Felicia, what have you been thinking?" "Felicia, please don't talk and I will have faith for you, because right now you are sad and weak." So a friend loves you at all times!!

I also know Crystal's strengths as well as her weaknesses and my love for her stirs a desire in me to never hurt her with my words. I can find no place in me to harm her or hold a grudge because I love her.

A friend never wants to harm you therefore; you must ask yourself how can an abuser be your true friend? It depends on your definition of a friend. A friend never ever wants to control your actions, bring any harm to you, or embarrass you. I have chosen a simple path which is to surround myself with people who seek to do me no harm in words or deeds. So seek simple math relationships love+giving=kindness. Life becomes easy when we stop making it so hard....1+1=2 and 2+2=4.

Mustard Seed Faith Vs Bitterness

Here is the key message I want to unfold to you today: the powerful force of faith vs. the evil venom of bitterness. In Matthew 17:20, Jesus told us we only needed a tiny measure of faith the size of a mustard seed for our faith to work. We give God a mustard seed amount of faith and it becomes a force He can do wonders with. However, the devil mimics that concept with the tiny little seed of bitterness. So if you have just a drop of bitterness left in your heart over a matter, it will give the devil a landing pad to begin his evil work inside of you.

I have noticed that whatever God sets in place, the devil plots to bring the opposing spirit to you in an evil deceptive manner. God wants your joy to be full as it gives you strength, but the devil wants you fearful, because it will hinder your faith.

Oh yes, the devil comes for anything in you that looks like his evil ways. The devil then thinks oh they want me in them, they are behaving like me, bitter and evil. From that little drop of bitter poison in your mind many things can grow. The following are a few behaviors and emotions that can grow in you: anger, resentment, jealousy, fear, hate, pride, evil meditations, or insecurity. Now you can see why we should never harbor a drop of bitterness in our heart. You just have to say "Lord, I forgive them".

I worked with a lady years ago who got mad at a staff member in her office. She would say I am not speaking to her anymore, roll her eyes, and turn her face in the opposite direction to not see her coworker and her face would actually get darker with a bitter ugly appearance. I said to her, "just forgive her" and she would say "nope, not talking to her". The office we worked at had a tiny parking lot and one way in the office. So you had to see each other all day long several times a day. I watched her do this ignoring routine for about a week. I finally said "look girl, let this go its making you look awful!!" I could see that the bitterness in her was growing to the point that her face actually looked like it would puff up when the lady would walk by. I will never forget seeing the effects of just a drop of bitterness from a simple misunderstanding the lady had with another person. It was a small, simple misunderstanding, but the scripture teaches us to not to let the sun go down on that type of bitter wrath in our hearts. This is a serious matter; bitter anger should be released from our hearts or thoughts every evening. I think it's powerful that God is so wise to let us know we should not even go to our beds at night with bitterness or anger in our hearts. This wise way of living will protect loving relationship towards our children, parents, siblings and spouse. Keep the faith of the grain of a mustard seed in your heart but never keep one little drop of bitterness in your heart. Let your faith always win over bitterness.

ALONE AT LAST!!

Being alone can be the most restful experience of your journey upon the end of a relationship. I made today's title one of excitement by using the exclamation symbols at the end. I did that because I wanted you to be excited about your alone time. Sure, there are moments of fear, doubt and loneliness, but your alone time is where you will find deep inner strength and clarity of mind. Why is this ALONE topic so major?? It's so major because what you do with this alone timeframe will determine your entire future. Your alone time now becomes a pivotal moment just like high school graduation was a pivotal moment in your life. You are on the path to get new mental pictures of who you are, make wise choices, set new goals, reach your objectives, have your mind filled with positive energy, and enjoy the peace each day desires to bring you. When you are solo you can do the most amazing things. Being in a healthy relationship is wonderful, but it takes energy and giving to accomplish that.

At the end of a relationship alone time is needed. People don't like being alone. They will fight hard to be with someone. I am not saying it's easy as 1,2 ,3 to be alone but it's a healthy thing to do. I will quickly say, don't feel sorry for yourself. Don't think negative thoughts about the future. The pain you feel now will go away. You will get stronger every day. Ohhhhh! Please don't over eat!! OMG why gain weight? You need to look cute because your ENTIRE life is about to go uphill from here!!

You will thank me later, if you follow my suggestion of having some alone time. Having an amazing person in your life is like finding an amazing dress. You don't buy the first dress you try on!! A time of deep inner reflection is needed; at the end of one relationship. It's healthy to look at your own goals; your God designed purpose, and what qualities you desire in a soul mate. Upon looking at all of these things, it's obvious how a person added into your life by God's divine timing will be a blessing.

Do you love music, travel and entertaining? Then why settle for a person who has no passport, no job, likes being alone and likes a quiet house. You will drive each other crazy!

Allow yourself this time to clear out old thoughts, lies and negative words spoken over you. A verbally abusive person seeks to make you feel you are constantly wrong and the problem is you. You will need the support of family and friends. Embrace being single and the wholeness which comes from your own inner peace. There is no one person that will ever bring inner joy and personal peace to you. You will only find peace within your own heart. This is when you will smile hearing the words, "Alone At last!! "I just want you to have joy about what God will produce in you as you are alone.

Part 2 tomorrow…

Alone at Last, Part 2!!

"For I know the plans I have for you, declares the Lord, plans to prosper you and not to harm you, plans to give you hope and a future." Jer 29:11 (NIV)

Your alone moments will bring a refreshing flow to your life in a speedy fashion. I am not saying you will feel no sadness or pain. You will get on the exact path for the journey and lessons you need to learn. Being alone takes away distractions, and allows space for the amazing healing that will emerge from this time of being alone. After five years of being alone, I am able to write this to you with joy of my growth. I would not change any part of it.

I want to share a few signs that you are becoming whole in your alone time. Here are a few things you will begin to do and experience with no pain or fear.

- Going to a movie alone
- Asking for a table for one at a fancy restaurant
- Driving to the beach alone
- Going to an elegant evening event alone looking cute!
- Taking care of your own auto repairs
- Finding new contacts for financial and business matters
- Organizing home repair needs
- Set up your spa day on your birthday
- Taking your summer vacation trip alone and you don't panic about being alone for the entire weekend. You wake up ready to enjoy the day!!
- You don't cry the entire weekend because you enjoy being your own best friend

When you do these powerful events alone it's not because you are a reject or unwanted. You have chosen this path of being alone to have the freedom to heal and be safe from the effects of abuse. The peace that comes over you is very rich and pleasantly overwhelming. You will also see your value. Others will see the peaceful healing that radiates from within you. Now, you see the joy of being alone at last. Breathe. Go get your coffee refilled.

While you are alone learn to love who you are and be good to yourself, first. Your atmosphere should be filled with goodness. When a negative person comes, they will not fit into your flow. Your peaceful flow will not allow them to stay around. You will kick that negative mess to the curb quick. Remember, when you began to work for your own money as a teenager? You placed value on your hard earned money. After being delivered from abuse, you worked hard for your healing. Value what you have worked for and make wise choices. The new healthy person in you will refute foolishness and negative drama. Enjoy your beautiful life. Enjoy all the blessing that will come. Look with great expectation, all the things God will add to your future...

THE CLEARING ZONE

Clearing is letting go of past hurts; painful thoughts, and forgiving those who have hurt you. You will now begin to heal and see that the all wise God is guiding you. He is directing the traffic of what leaves your life and what comes into your life. When you clear your spirit, your healing with occur in a more rapid pace. New relationships take energy to build and you don't have that energy yet. You have got to trust me...

I don't believe in crying over a person who is rude. I may cry over a hurtful thought but I refuse to cry over the abuser. You are in the clearing zone so you have to let go of things that clutter your mental space or drain your energy.

When you release an abusive person from your life I feel they no longer have a place of honor in your life. They don't honor you. They don't respect you; their words or actions have shown you that. More than likely, they have moved on to their next relationship. Please honor yourself in the clearing zone. Release them from your emotional life. This is why I say don't cry for them or be lonely for them. Above all things don't continue a sexual relationship with the abusive person, even if you are still married. This would be confusing and I don't advise it. Don't even have a coffee date. You're done!!

It's time to honor your life and well being. Why make love to a rude person or eat a meal with them? No longer will you give them the message that you don't honor your own life. The clearing zone also has a new stage for you to set. You pick the new boundaries that will be respected. Boundaries are used to keep good things in and block bad things out. Think about a fence. You pick what's inside the fence. You can even lock the fence. You are the only person with the key. Enjoy this part of you healing; because it's an important stage you are about to set. The clearing zone is also a time to decrease the power and influence of the abuser. I started a term called fasting words. Instead of abstaining from food, you go without speaking a particular word. When you do a word fast, it can be a name; a lingering fearful thought, or a past hurtful event. You get to set the stage to meet your needs as you heal. I chose to no longer say the name of my former spouse not out of bitterness but it took away his influence. I selected to not speak his name in my new healed environment because he lost a place of honor in my life. As I did the 'word fast,' I then noticed several days would pass and I would not even think of my former spouse. The next fast was hurtful events. The event was no longer discussed or thought of. I did personal professional counseling; grieved the lost of a marriage, learned what abusive behavior was. Then I released it all. The 'word fast' became a powerful tool in the clearing zone.

Rain on your face is about healing, cleansing, clearing out negative thoughts and enjoying your new inner growth. You are alive with a beautiful life ahead of you. Learn to live in the present every day. Don't live in the past and don't try to live in the future or you will miss out on the wonderful plan of TODAY. I have found that each day has something lovely to offer me. I realize that even in a challenging moment or in a difficult time, the challenge itself is a blessing. The challenge gives me the opportunity to obtain strength and new profound growth.

Enjoy the clearing because it is quite powerful. You will experience new ideals.   New thoughts emerge from the quietness of your healed calm heart. Take time to reflect on things you want to let go of. Set new boundaries you want to structure in the clearing zone. What a powerful moment of choice is before you, today. You are now in the zone, and it's the clearing zone.

SHADOWS AND FALSE ILLUSIONS

We can all remember the very first time we saw our own shadow. Shadows need light, and then something to obscure the light to create the shadow. Even though the shadow looks tall, big, or dark the shadow can't harm you. One interesting fact is when the source of light is further away; the object that creates the shadow will become much larger. I call the shadow an illusion of the truth that has blocked the light. In the light we find clarity, better vision, and a better sense of factual truth.

Abusive people are so far from God in their thinking. They also like to stand over you when they talk, and this is done to cast their gloomy shadow over you. This shadow blocks the light of God's truth. Their gloomy shadow towering over you is done to dominate you and create fear. They are trying to imitate God. Their shadow brings no comforting strength nor does it have true power.

Psalms 91 Says he that dwells in the secret place shall abide under the shadow of the almighty. The next thing we see in verse 2 is: I will say of the Lord, He is my refuge and my fortress, my God, in whom I trust. The shadow of the Lord is really the shelter, shade, and comfort of God.

Come away from the abusers' shadow that is being cast over you; and the illusion of fear in any abusive situation. Don't shrink into the darkness of the abusive actions; or words you may find yourself in at this time. In the darkest situation God's light is so big. He will guide you out of the darkness into the light. Then the only power over you is the Lord. Take comfort from God as you abide in the shadow of the almighty. May you only see the great shadow of God's protective love over you.

WHAT DID YOU JUST SAY?

As you add new friends to your life really listen to what they say. It is amazing to me the things people will say with a straight face, yet no honor of God in their heart. What I want to share is a bit difficult to even write or say it, but I have to. When you hear a person say something wrong over and over with no fear of God, be very careful of that person.

If a man says this famous jingle; I am a grown Ass man he is not in connection with God. If he says it, just say to him,"what did you just say?" Just making sure you heard it.

Okay, class is now in session. Let me teach you what he really means. He thinks it a cute way of saying he's an adult. He is not honoring God. When he says, "I am a grown Ass man," he is not having respect for his own life, to say that. He is actually creating a strong hold over his own mind. He is starting a process to divide and harden his heart; which will prevent him from hearing God. This is a set up that will harm many areas of his life. He is drastically defeating his ability to be a leader in his home. He is weakening his ability to mentor his children. There is a hindrance in the growth to love a wife. If he really knew the effects of these words, he would stop saying it. These words destroy the family and causes arguments which can even lead to divorce. This continues the awful cycle of poor examples of love in a family.

The grown 'Ass man' can't mentor his sons. He can't be tender to his daughters to show them the love of a father. The grown 'ass man' raises children who are broken. They have a weak understanding about love, true sacrifice, and unconditional love. They never actually see the demonstration of healthy family behaviors; of unity and kindness in a home setting. His sons repeat his bad rude behaviors and his daughters tolerates rude behaviors from another grown 'ass man' when she leaves home.

I thank God for the loving man my father was and it gave me the strength to get out and walk away. My dad was kind and talked to me with deep respect. He did not use profanity nor did he ever spank me. He would only verbally correct me. The role of a father is very powerful to a woman.

Words have a spirit that comes with them that affect our behavior. For example, if you say "I'm scared," over and over, you get nervous and feel horrible. If you say, "I'm ok. It's all good," you get calm.

This will be a study of words and behavior. Let's start with an over view of the grown 'Ass man.' He is telling you the following things will be some of his behaviors.

- He makes his own rules.
- He is not concerned about scripture
- He has a huge ego
- He is a poor listener
- He is god
- He rarely prays
- It's extremely difficult for him to apologize

- He don't check in with nobody
- His actions will be based on how he feels at the moment
- He will do things for you, IF its convent for him
- He's late for appointment
- He will not check on your needs
- He will make plans and break them
- He speaks without concern of the outcome of his words
- He might cuss you out. After all, he's a grown 'ASS man!!'
- This man has no inner compass from God for his actions or his words
- His ego gets more inflated as he quotes the jingle; I'm a grown 'ass man '
- He will quote that when he is clearly wrong and not in a position to be corrected by God's spirit. In fact he can't hear God, so he sure ain't gonna hear you!!
- He is in an adult body with the decision making ability of an 8-12 year old boy or maybe at best a 20 year old
- Oh he believes in God and he goes to church but his heart is distant from God
- He can't give you scripture to back up how he lives
- He does know the scripture; wives obey your husband and women should be obedient

Many times he has not had the example of a godly man loving a woman. He may not have ever seen a man be respectful to a woman. There is also the pressure from other grown 'ASS men', he has to impress because they all feel this is what being a real man is. Now, we will do a word study according to the free dictionary app. Let's just look at the word and what it really means

Definition of ass: stupid or asinine. A vulgar slang used to mean a rectum or sexual acts.

Adjectives: asinine, obstinate (stubborn/stiff-necked) or stupid, utterly stupid or silly. Asinine behavior (devoid of intelligence)

Synonyms: mindless, foolish, devoid of good senses or judgment. Foolish remarks, foolish decisions.

Also you will see the synonym moronic to describe ass. Moronic is very taboo to use but years ago it was used to describe people with mental issues who function with the mind of an 8-12 year old. A grown 'ASS man' has just been defined above. Let's do a summary. When a man chants that jingle, he is really saying the following: he's stupid, asinine, a rectum, stubborn, stiff-necked, utterly stupid or silly, devoid of good senses or judgment, makes foolish remarks, mindless and moronic having the mind of a 8-12 year old.

Now, in fairness all men don't say they are grown 'ASS men'. I believe in being healthy to speak life and truth about good men. Let's look at the Antonyms to Ass which is the opposite meaning: bright, smart, wise, intelligent, sensible and sane. Ahhh! that sounds much better. Ok I'm done your have been warned!!!

You are looking for a man after God's path. You are looking for a man that lives by 1 Corinthians 13:4-7. The 1 Corinthians 13 man knows love is patient and takes no delight in evil. This man's words will be a reflection of God's Word. He is corrected by God.

THAT'S NOT MY LUGGAGE

In your new life of healing, always be clear on who you really are. No voices from the past will ever define you. God defines you. You agree with God not any negative things spoken over you.

When you are at the airport, you see lots of luggage. Sometimes, you think you see your luggage. However, when you walk up to it you say inwardly "that's not my luggage." There is something that only you know that identifies your piece of luggage. When you see various pieces of luggage on the carousel, you wait for your luggage. You would never roll three pieces of luggage belonging to another person, out to your car.

You don't take baggage that does not belong to you! The message I want to leave you with is don't take the baggage of words abusive people try to give you. Don't take one piece of old, beat up, abused and mix matched baggage that try tried to place in your possession. You are not the owner of those sad, lied filled suit cases. They are trying to load you down with tons of unnecessary extra weight that is not your luggage!! When you travel, you have to pay for overweight luggage. So, travel light and in a first class seat. You never belonged in coach to start with!!

Leave the old luggage behind and move on with your life. Move on with your designer luggage filled with your own new truths and strength for the journey ahead. Happy travels and have a safe flight. Go. Enjoy your new world.

GUIDED JOURNALING INSTRUCTIONS FROM THE HEALING COACH

This section is designed to give you deeper insight into your inner thoughts, to avoid mental meltdowns, to look at healthy vs unhealthy relationships and to self design your action plans. So, the guided journaling will lead you to your new mindsets, help you understand negative mental triggers and assist you with a written plan to bring stability to your life. The healing path is now before you and may you enjoy your life filled with intentional plans. You should review these plans frequently to hold yourself accountable. I pray abundant blessings on the plans you are about to design.

What makes you feel peaceful? What makes your home environment calm? List these ideals and in moments of frustration or worry come to this page.

Who do you call in your darkest moments? If you feel a mental meltdown starting do you have their number/email written down? (In case you have cell phone/computer malfunction)

If you are currently in a relationship, what are the healthy or unhealthy aspects of that relationship? Do you feel safe and if not what is your plan to get out.

What motivates you to reach new goals? What are the next 3 Goals for your life?

List your 5 closest friends and the value they add to your life. Are they a reflection of the goals and values you have? If not how will you solve this?

What books are you reading to enhance your healing? What topics can you Google for self awareness to advance your healing?

What are you doing to maintain good physical health? Focus on this with great care and be aware that setting up this plan actually shows you love yourself. Remember to do your annual health screens and Mammograms.

What is the common reoccurring negative ideal that attacks you mentally? (Remember it's a "Lie Vision")

Do you know the triggers that make you feel sad or worried? It could be words, ideals, places or holidays. List them and have intentional plans to silence the trigger words or events.

What is your 21 day plan to break a bad habit or let go of an unhealthy relationship?

Who is your mentor? What are 5 things they have instructed you to do? Mentoring comes from deep love and dedication, so value their instruction. They see what you may not be able to see yet.

What are the positive things you like about yourself? (Paint the beautiful picture of who you are Beautiful Girl !!)

How do you care for your emotional life and stress reduction? When was your last spa visit or vacation away from your home? Where is your next travel destination? (Dream Big)

Who are the Spiritual Leaders in your life? What are the 5 basic instructions or inspiration they have given you?

Scriptures for Comfort

I found great comfort from scripture and seeing Gods perspective on various issues. Below I will share issues you may face and scripture references that help me heal and grow stronger. You should make it a top priority to set aside personal time to read the suggested scriptures. You will be surprised how other verses will get your attention as you read. Scripture reading is a wonderful way to clear your mind, renew your thinking patterns and get the clarity you need for your life.

- God will protect you and guide you out of the difficult places in your life. (Read Psalms 19:1-2 and9-11)

- God will support you and sustain you. (Read Psalms55:22)

- Submit your life to God and don't worry when you can't figure out how to handle a situation.(Read Proverbs3:5-6)

- You can't fix a person's behavior but you can remove yourself form unhealthy relationships.(Read Proverbs 3:7-8)

- Mentors give you wise counsel listen to them. Trust that God has sent them to your life.(Read Proverbs 3:13-17

- Don't allow anger to make you use profanity. Refuse to argue seek peaceful relationships.(Read Ephesians 4:29-33)

- Don't worry about what things you lose. Find safety for your life.(Read Proverbs 16:8)

- Refuse to let bitterness be in your heart it's harmful to all areas of your life. (Read Hebrews 12:15)

- Commit your life and all plans to God he will work out every detail for you.(read Proverbs 16:3-4)

- Don't worry when people have harmed you and they look successful.(Read Proverbs 3:31)

- Use each day to improve your life and sow good seed of kindness and make sure your actions are honorable. God will make sure blessing come back to you.(Read Galatians 6:7-9)

- Never allow hate to be in your heart. It darkens your thoughts and hinders spiritual growth. (Read 1John 1:5-7)

- When a person does unkind acts God is not in their heart and they can't see Gods way to love you.(Read 1John 2:9-11)

- Remain humble as you move on with your life you have nothing to prove to others and just sit back and let God lift you up again.(Read James 4:10)

SUPPORT HOTLINE AND SUGGESTED BOOK REFERENCES

National Domestic Violence Hotline 1-800-787-3224.

24hour Support Line 1-800-799-7233

Call the support line if you need to talk to someone. Help is available 24/7 365 days a year. Talk to experienced advocates they can discuss resources or provide information to help you understand unhealthy relationships.

Their website is www.thehotline.org/help on this site you can read expert advice and see other resources that are available.

Suggested Books to read

1) Why Does he do that? Inside the mind of angry controlling men) by Lundy Bancroft.

2) Should I stay or should I go? By Lundy Bancroft

3) When Dad Hurts Mom: Helping children heal the wounds of witnessing abuse. By Lundy Bancroft

Lundy explains abuse and the reasons for abusive behavior in a way that will forever change your life. You will feel like you have had hours of counseling after reading. Visit his web site for additional information at www.lundybancroft.com

About The Author

Felicia is a dynamic speaker, mentor, and healing coach. A season of disappointing events in her life became the fuel to propel her into seeking knowledge on emotional healing. She found faith in God's perspective over her life and she calls God the ultimate healer of all things. Her personal interest include planting flowers, listening to classical music, Art gallery tours, fancy coffeehouses, organizing vacation packages and her favorite destination is any place in the Caribbean. She also has an absolute fascination with using Google to study topics or words.

She is a passionate worship dancer in a duet ministry called Purified Gold and dances with her best friend Crystal. Purified Gold Worship Ministry's travels have been across the USA, London, Puebla, Mexico, and the Islands of the Bahamas, Barbados and Jamaica. She is the Founder and Director of a 501C 3 Non-Profit public charity called American Life Caribbean Mission. Her Mission is mentoring students in Trench Town, providing scholarships to students at the UWI and she keeps connections with the graduates to encourage them to mentor others.

Felicia is a graduate of North Carolina Central University and she has a Bachelor's of Science degree in Nursing. She attended Emory Medical in Atlanta, Georgia to become a Certified Wound Nurse Specialist. Her current role in nursing is providing consultations and knowledge to heal physical wounds. She is the Author of Rain on Your Face and seeks to help others heal now in their emotional needs. She believes when we spread love only then are we reflections of God's kindness and forgiveness is the best seed you can sow.

CONTENTS AND GUIDANCE

If you feel weary read one section. Fill your mind with something positive from any page below. I'm praying for you and God is with you. Fill your mind with new positive thoughts it's the key to healing.

Acknowledgements...1

Beautiful Girl...2

Rain On Your Face..3

Doing Your Homework To Heal...5

Fears To Release And Goals To Achieve 6

What In The World Went Wrong? 9

New Revelations And Self Validation 10

It's Time To Stop Crying..12

The Chipped Seashell...13

God's Cleansing Rain...14

Deception 16

Lie Vision 17

Removed From The Grip Of Evil 19

What Is God Saying To You?..20

No Not Today!..22

Musical Quiet Zone 24

Cappuccino Moment..25

Be Careful What Your Little Ears Hear..26

Making A Pot Of Simmering Chili...27

Intentional Actions..29

Be Wise And Know God's Will 30

Physical And Financial Stability...31

Climb The Ladder...33

Who's Going To Love Me? 34

Activities To Nurture My Life 36

Chocolate Cake 37

Lord Navigate My Mind...38

The Fear Cycle 41

Saying I Love You 42

Tranquil Mind 43

You Are Not Lonely You Have Yourself 44

Pack You're About To Move! 45

Proverbs Chapter 2 46

Right Thing Wrong Season 47

Change Your Nail Polish 48

Single Red Rose 49

Abusers Are Not Your Friend 50

Mustard Seed Faith Vs Bitterness 51

Alone At Last!! 52

Alone At Last Part 2!! 53

The Clearing Zone 54

Shadows And False Illusions 56

What Did You Just Say? 57

That's Not My Luggage 59